Who Laid the
Cornerstone
of the World?

Ann Pilling

Illustrated by Helen Cann

Loyola Press

Chicago

For Christine Swart—A.P.
For Sarah Welply—H.C.

First published in North America in 2000 by
Loyola Press
3441 North Ashland Avenue
Chicago, Illinois 60657

This edition © 1999 by Lion Publishing, plc
Selection and retellings © 1999 by Ann Pilling
Illustrations © 1999 by Helen Cann
All rights reserved

Originally published by Lion Publishing, plc, Oxford,
England

Acknowledgments
The story text has been adapted from the Bible. Some
excerpts from specific translations have been used:

Bible passages on pp. 21, 22, 23 quoted from the Good News
Bible, published by The Bible Societies/HarperCollins
Publishers Ltd, UK; © 1966, 1971, 1976, 1992 by American
Bible Society. Used by permission.

Bible passages on pp. 32, 35, 42 quoted from the
International Children's Bible, New Century Version
(Anglicized Edition) © 1991 by Nelson Word Ltd, Milton
Keynes, England. Used by permission.

Bible passage on p. 23 quoted from the New Jerusalem Bible
© 1985 by Darton, Longman & Todd, Ltd., and Doubleday,
a division of Bantam Doubleday Dell, Inc. Reprinted by
permission.

Words to "Great Is Thy Faithfulness" by Thomas O.
Chisholm, © 1951 by Hope Publishing. Administered by
CopyCare, PO Box 77, Hailsham, BN27 3EF, UK. Used by
permission.

Design by Nicky Farthing

ISBN 0-8294-1485-1

Printed and bound in Singapore
00 01 02 03 04 / 10 9 8 7 6 5 4 3 2 1

Introduction

The title of this collection is a question put to Job by God himself, and it is the sort of basic question asked by every child: "Who made me and where did everything come from?" "What happens when we die?" "How did evil get into a perfect world?" "Why do people have to suffer?" These are not childish questions; they are only childlike. The child in each of us never stops asking them.

These stories, drawn from the Old and New Testaments of the Bible, have been chosen because they raise such questions and provide answers, though these are sometimes unexpected and mysterious.

They are not history or straight theological teaching; they are colorful and dramatic stories capable of persuading and instructing in a way nothing else can. Some of Jesus' most powerful teaching was given in parables.

The stories have been retold for children. This calls for simple language, but I have tried to preserve the dignity and beauty of the seventeenth-century Bible translations that are so much a part of our heritage. The tale of Jonah's running away

from God and grumpily sitting under a vine is not without humor.

There is something endearing, also, in the way Job argues so earnestly with his Creator before falling silent in the face of his very greatness.

The themes of the stories vary considerably, ranging from the muddle of languages at Babel to the angel who preserved the three brothers from the flames; from God's destruction of his own world out of grief at man's wickedness to Jesus' puzzling tale of the seed that dies. Yet the same image seems to embrace them all. It is of a God who, though endlessly varied and mysterious, has manifested the same characteristics to all people throughout all ages. The God of Jonah and Noah and Job is the God of Jesus also, a God of mercy and a God of love.

Contents

In the Beginning

*The story of creation and
why the world exists*

In the beginning, there was only God, and his Spirit moved over the face of the dark waters like a great bird, brooding over the deep where everything was darkness and confusion. This awful nothingness was called chaos.

God ended the darkness by saying, "Let there be light." And there was light. He had only to utter his command and it was done. All things came into being through God. He created everything there is.

When God saw that the light he had made was good, he began to make the world. He made every part of it: the enormous things and the tiny things and the in-between things. He took great care with everything because he was a loving God who wanted his world to be perfect in every detail.

He began with the enormous things, separating the light he had made from the darkness that had been there before. He created day and night, and when he had made the first morning and evening, the first day of creation was over.

On the second day, God made a firmament, a vault of sky that arched above the waters. He was like a silversmith beating out a great shining panel; like a tentmaker spreading a roof over the world. He called the vault heaven, and by the time this work was done, it was evening again. The second day of creation was over.

On the third day, God did many more things. He gathered all the waters together and made them into seas. "Let the dry land appear," he said. And it was so. On the earth he caused green things to start growing: plants that would bear seeds and trees that would bear fruit. Everything had within itself the beginnings of more life. God created the world in such a way that things could multiply all on their own. And he saw that this was very good indeed.

Next, God turned to the firmament he had made, and he adorned it like an artist. How beautiful it became as his loving hands created two great lights that he hung in the sky like lamps, one to rule the day and the other to rule the night. He made these lights, which are our sun and moon, to give the earth its different seasons, not just day and night. He made the stars also. Evening came once again and then another morning. The fourth day of creation was over, but God had not yet finished.

On the fifth day, he set about making all kinds of living creatures, and he was extravagant. He created millions of everything: swarms of sea creatures to fill the deep and flocks of fowl to fly above them in the sky. Some of these creatures were so tiny that they looked like specks of brilliant light. Everything, whether great or small, belonged to its own species and was separate from the next. Everything had its own special way of life. Although God had made countless numbers of creatures, he knew every single one of them.

Then, on the sixth day, he did even more. He made all the animals, and like the birds and the sea creatures, they were very different from each other. Some walked, and some crept. Some were fast, and some were slow. Some were big, some were small, and some were in between. God looked at the teeming earth, now full to overflowing with marvelous life, and he saw that it was very good.

But one thing still remained. At last God said, "Let us make man in our own

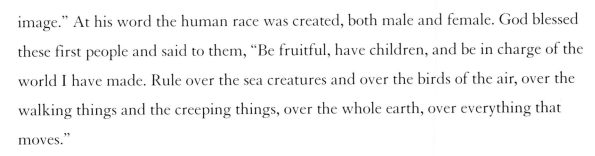

image." At his word the human race was created, both male and female. God blessed these first people and said to them, "Be fruitful, have children, and be in charge of the world I have made. Rule over the sea creatures and over the birds of the air, over the walking things and the creeping things, over the whole earth, over everything that moves."

God forgot nothing he had created. He wanted the human beings to look after everything carefully, for he had made it carefully. "Everything has food provided for it to eat," he told them. "There are green and growing things for my creatures, and plants and trees will yield their seeds and fruit so that you will have plenty."

After his work was done, God looked at everything he had made and saw that it was very good. And the evening and the morning were the sixth day.

Everything was finished now—the earth and the sky and everything that is in them. More wonderful things had been made by God in those six days than there are grains of sand on the seashore. So on the seventh day he was wise. He did nothing at all but rest. In this way the seventh day of the week became a special day, a sabbath when all things could copy their Creator and rest with him. They could look with him at the beautiful world he had made and enjoy it.

So it was God who laid the cornerstone of the world and made everything there is. See how carefully he did it, how he provided everything his creatures needed, knowing they would need both rest and play as well as food and drink.

It is hard to understand how the Creator, who made huge things like the sun, the moon, and the stars, could take the same care over the little things, and know all his creatures one by one. Yet he did, and he does, because he is Love.

The spacious firmament on high,

With all the blue ethereal sky,

And spangled heavens, a shining frame,

Their great original proclaim.

The unwearied sun, from day to day,

Does his Creator's power display;

And publishes to every land

The work of an almighty hand. . . .

What though in solemn silence all

Move round this dark terrestrial ball;

What though no real voice or sound

Amid their radiant orbs be found:

In reason's ear they all rejoice,

And utter forth a glorious voice,

For ever singing as they shine:

"The hand that made us is divine!"

Joseph Addison (1672–1719)

The Wily Serpent

*The story of Adam and Eve and
why there is both good and bad*

The very first people on earth were called Adam and Eve. Adam came first, and God made him from the dust of the ground. He breathed into his nostrils, and the man became a living soul. In the East, in a place called Eden, God planted a tree-filled garden for Adam to live in. These trees were beautiful to look at, and they also bore fruit. All God's trees were lovely, but the loveliest of all were the two he placed in the middle of his garden. These were called the Tree of Life and the Tree of the Knowledge of Good and Evil.

God knew that all growing things need water, so he created a great river to flow through the garden. This river separated into four more rivers that flowed out into the world: Pishon, which was rich with the finest gold, Gihon, Euphrates, and Tigris. The very names of the rivers sound like music.

God had placed Adam in the garden of Eden so that he could work there and look after it. He was to be God's gardener. He was free to do whatever he liked—except for one thing. God, who knew what was best for his creatures, told him that he must not eat any fruit from the Tree of the Knowledge of Good and Evil. "If you do this," God told him, "then you will die."

Now God knew that it was not good for the man to be alone, so he thought to himself, "I will make him a helper." But first he brought before Adam the different animals he had created and told him to name them all. Whatever Adam called the animal, that became its name. In this way, God entrusted to the man the care of all the creatures he had made.

The animals had each other but there was nobody to help Adam. God caused Adam to fall into a deep sleep, and taking a rib bone out of his body and closing up the flesh again, he fashioned a woman. When Adam woke, God showed her to him. "She is bone of my bone and flesh of my flesh," the man said. This is why, when a man and a woman love each other, they become husband and wife. From then on they belong to each other, and without each other they are not complete. This is because when God created the very first man and woman, they shared the same flesh and bone.

As they walked together in God's beautiful garden, they were naked, but they did not feel ashamed of their bodies. They were happy.

But this happiness did not last. In the garden, quite unknown to them, there was a wicked creature bent upon doing evil who had disguised himself in the form of a serpent. This creature, more crafty than any other animal that God had made, sidled up to the woman and said, "Did God really forbid you to eat fruit from the Tree of the Knowledge of Good and Evil?"

The woman was innocent. She did not understand that the serpent was trying to cast doubt on God's loving purposes. "Yes," she told him. "If we eat that fruit or touch that tree, we will die."

"That is not true," the crafty serpent said. "You will not die. God has only forbidden you to touch the tree because if you eat of its fruit you will know good and evil, like he does; in fact, you will become just as powerful."

The woman thought about this and looked at the tree. The beautiful ripe fruit was very tempting to eat, but she was also tempted by the thought of becoming as wise as God. So she stretched out her hand, plucked some of the fruit, and ate it. Then she gave some to her husband, and he ate it too. As they enjoyed the delicious fruit together, their eyes were opened for the first time. They understood all things, and they knew that they were naked. Taking leaves from a fig tree, they sewed them together to cover themselves. Meanwhile, the serpent vanished silently into the trees.

It was evening, and the Lord God was walking in his garden in the cool of the day. Hearing him, they hid, but God called out, "Adam, where are you?"

The man and the woman came out of their hiding place and stood before God. "I hid when I heard your voice," Adam said, "because I knew that I was naked and I felt ashamed."

"Who told you that you were naked?" God asked. "Have you eaten fruit from the forbidden tree?"

Adam hung his head. "It was the woman you provided to be my helper," he said. "She gave me the fruit."

So God turned to the woman. "What is this thing you have done?" he asked her.

She, too, could not look at God. "A serpent came," she said. "He deceived me. That is why I ate the forbidden fruit."

Then God cursed the serpent. "From now on," he said, "you will crawl along the ground and you will eat nothing but dust. I will make you and these human creatures enemies forever and ever. They will tread on you and crush your head, but in return you will sting them in the heel."

To the woman God said, "When you bear children, you will be in pain, and the man whose helper you were meant to be will now rule over you."

To Adam he said, "Because you ate the forbidden fruit, the earth I made for you to enjoy will become your enemy. It will fill up with thorns and thistles, and to get food from it you will have to sweat and toil all the days of your life. This will go on till you die. I made you from dust, and to dust you will return."

Then Adam turned to his wife and gave her the name "Eve" because she was to become the mother of the human race.

God knew that Adam and Eve could not stay with him anymore. "If they were to eat from the Tree of Life," he said, "they would live forever." So he made them clothes out of animal skins to protect them against the harsh world beyond the garden, and he sent them away to labor in it. At the entrance to his garden he placed an angel with a flaming sword that flashed this way and that, guarding the path that led to the Tree of Life.

That is why there is both bad and good in the world, when God meant there to be only good. He had given Adam and Eve freedom, which meant that they were free to choose bad things as well as good, and they chose to do bad. But God went on providing for them, even as he sent them off to work in the world beyond Eden.

As Adam and Eve walked away hand in hand, God watched them from the entrance to his garden, and he looked sad.

The Promise of the Rainbow

*The story of Noah, which tells
of God's love and faithfulness*

God had created a perfect world, but evil had entered it. Soon it was full of wickedness. There was violence and there was murder. Nothing at all was as God had planned.

When he saw how the whole world was bent on doing evil, his heart filled with pain. He was sorry that he had ever created the human race. He said, "I will wipe it from the face of the earth and with it every other creature that I have made. I grieve now that I created any of them." But there was one man on earth whom God still loved. His name was Noah, and this is his story.

Noah was a righteous man who walked with God, and it was to Noah that God confided his plan to destroy the earth. "Because you are the one good man in a world of very wicked people," he said, "I am going to save you.

"You must build a boat, big enough for you and your family and for a male and a female of every kind of creature that I have created. There must be room for food also, enough to feed both you and the animals." Then God explained to Noah how he should construct the boat and he gave him the exact measurements. "Make it out of cypress wood," he said. "Build a lot of rooms, and coat the boat with pitch inside and out to make it watertight. Give it three decks. Put a door in the side and a roof on top. When you are all inside, I will make it rain for forty days and forty nights. Apart from you, everything I have created will be drowned."

Noah did exactly what God said and set about constructing an enormous boat—an ark—on dry land. To those who stood watching, it must have seemed a foolish thing to do, but Noah trusted God completely.

When the ark was finished, he went inside with his wife and his children. All the animals came to Noah asking to be let in, so he admitted a male and a female of each kind as he had been told to do. And the Lord God shut them in.

Then the rain came. The springs of the deep burst forth, the floodgates of heaven were opened, and it rained without stopping for forty days and forty nights, just as God had said. The flood was gigantic. The water rose steadily until it covered the mountaintops; then it went on rising. Everything God had made was destroyed—every bird, every animal, every human being. Only Noah was left and those who were with him in the ark, which bobbed about on the heaving flood in perfect safety. God had judged the evil world sternly, but he had been a loving father to Noah because Noah had been obedient.

For 150 days the world was covered with water. There were no signs of life because everything had perished. It was just as it had been in the awful chaos time before the world was made.

But God remembered Noah.

God caused a wind to blow across the earth, driving the waters back. Little by little the floods retreated and began to go down. This took many months, but one day Noah realized that the ark had come to rest somewhere. It was on top of a mountain called Ararat.

He waited for forty days before opening a window. He sent out a raven, which flew to and fro over the earth. Then he sent out a dove, but there was no dry place on which she could rest, so he stretched out his hand and brought her back into the safety of the ark. The second time he sent the dove out, she came back with a freshly picked olive branch in her beak. This was wonderful because it was proof that things had started to grow again. The third time he sent her out, the dove did not return.

Many more days passed. Inside the ark, Noah waited patiently to hear God's word. Only when the floodwaters had dried up completely and he saw that the ground was dry did the Lord speak to him. "Come out of the ark," he said. "You and your family and all the creatures with you. Everything must have young and multiply." It was just as if the world were being created all over again.

Noah's very first act was to say "thank you" to God for saving them all. He built an altar to the Lord and made sacrifices upon it, and God smelled a sweet smell as the smoke rose into the sky.

Then he said, "Never again will I curse this earth of mine. Never again will I destroy all living creatures. While the earth remains, seedtime and harvest, and cold and heat, and summer and winter shall not cease."

Every year, from that time on, the seasons would come and go and come back again. Human beings knew that they could rely on this pattern, that they could trust God not to change anything. They knew that he would remain faithful.

God blessed Noah and his family and all the animals, and he made a solemn promise, a promise called a covenant: "Never again will I destroy the earth with a

flood," he said. "And as a sign of my covenant, I am going to hang my bow in the sky. It will not be a bow that shoots arrows, a weapon of war; it will be a beautiful thing, a sign of peace. It will be a rainbow. Whenever I see it, shining through the clouds, I will remember that I have made this promise to you. It is a sign of the everlasting covenant between me and all life on earth."

To this day, when rainbows appear in the sky, they remind people of the story of Noah and of God's love and faithfulness.

Great is Thy faithfulness, O God my Father,
There is no shadow of turning with Thee. . . .
All I have needed Thy hand hath provided,
Great is Thy faithfulness, Lord, unto me!

Thomas O. Chisholm (1866–1960)

The Tower That Reached to Heaven

*The story of the tower of Babel and why
people find it hard to understand one another*

There are thousands of different languages in the world, and in order to understand one another, people have to learn them. This is hard work, but it was not always like this. The story of the tower that reached to heaven tells what went wrong.

In ancient times, the people who had survived the flood spoke just one language. It was a simple one with very few words. As they increased in number, they started to look for somewhere to make their home. At last, in a place called Shinar, they discovered a great plain. They decided to stop there and settle down. They were builders, and they had great plans.

First they said to each other, "Let us make bricks. Let us bake them until they are good and hard and fix them together with tar." There was no stone in Shinar and what they planned to build had to last, so the bricks had to be very hard indeed. Then they said, "Let us build ourselves a city, a city with a tower so high that it reaches to the heavens, so that we can make a name for ourselves and be important, in case we are scattered all over the earth." These people wanted to be the envy of the world.

In his court in heaven, God was listening to them. He decided to go to the city and see the great tower. He already knew what would come of these plans. He said, "If these people, who speak only one language, are already trying to reach heaven by building a tower, then they will stop at nothing. Come, let us go down to earth and confuse their speech, so that they will no longer understand each other." He knew that the builders of the tower were very ambitious. They trusted in their own skills and wanted to run their own lives. There was no room for God at all. He wanted to show them that human beings cannot be like God, nor can they reach him by building a tower so big that it reaches the sky.

So he scattered them. He scattered them all over the earth, and the tower and the city were never finished. After this there were always hundreds of different languages in the world, and it became harder and harder for people to understand one another. The abandoned city was called Babel because it was there that God muddled up human speech, turning it into a kind of babble.

It was not in God's plan to confuse speech like this, but he scattered and confused the proud builders of that tower in order to take away their pride and their ambition. It was to teach them to rely more on him and less on themselves.

The Day Everything Went Wrong

*The story of Job and how bad things
happen to good people*

Job, who lived in the land of Uz, was a God-fearing man. He lived a good life, and there was no evil in him. Job had seven sons and three daughters. He had many servants and no end of sheep, camels, oxen, and donkeys. He sometimes worried about his children and would make sacrifices on their behalf, in case they were doing evil things and cursing God. Job himself was righteous, the greatest man in the East.

One day, Satan paid God a visit in the courts of heaven, and they had a conversation. "What have you been doing?" God asked.

"Roaming around the earth," said Satan. (It was his chief business to cause people to break God's laws.)

Then God said, "Have you considered my servant Job? He is most righteous of men"

"Yes, but he doesn't fear you for nothing," Satan answered. "And he only blesses you because you have made him rich. If he became poor, he would not bless you then; he would curse you."

"All right," God said. "Do whatever you like to him, but do not lay a finger on the man himself."

So Satan left the court and set about ruining Job's life.

And he succeeded. People kept coming to Job with terrible news. First he heard that the Sabeans, an enemy people, had killed all his oxen and all his donkeys. Then came news that his sheep and his servants had been consumed by fire. Next he was told that a whirlwind had hit the house where his children were feasting and that every single one of them was dead.

But Job did not curse God. He simply said, "The Lord gave and the Lord has taken away; blessed be the name of the Lord," and he continued to worship him.

So Satan went back to the courts of heaven. "I was right," God said. "Job does not curse me, in spite of all his troubles."

"Ah yes," replied Satan. "But at least he's still alive. If terrible things were done to his body, he would definitely curse you then."

"Very well," said God. "He is in your hands. Do whatever you want to him, but do not actually kill him."

So Satan covered Job with hideous sores from head to foot. To try and get some relief Job went and sat on a heap of ashes and scraped himself with a bit of broken pottery. His wife jeered at him. "Still living the good life, husband?" she cried. "Curse God, and die!"

"You speak like a fool," Job said. "Should we accept only good things from God? Should we not accept bad things too?"

Job had three friends: Eliphaz, Bildad, and Zophar. When they heard about his troubles, they set off together to try and comfort him. But when they saw him, they wept and tore their clothes. He was unrecognizable, and his pain seemed endless. For seven days and seven nights they did not speak at all; they merely sat beside him on the ground.

When at last Job opened his mouth, he still did not curse God, but by now his many sufferings had quite worn him down. "Cursed be the day I was born!" he said. "Why did I not perish at birth? Why do those who want to die have to go on living?"

"Don't give up hope," lectured Eliphaz. "We all have to suffer. In fact, man is born to have trouble just as surely as the sparks fly upward. God lets us suffer from time to time old friend, but he always bandages our wounds up afterward." This sounded

quite comforting. Then Eliphaz added, "It's really God's way of punishing you, all this trouble of yours. If you take my advice, you'll pull yourself together."

Some friend he was!

Bildad was worse. "Stop complaining, you old windbag," he began. "All right, so your children have died. Well, I'm sorry, but it's probably your own fault. When people have done wrong, evil lies in wait for them like a hungry monster ready to gobble them up. God is so great and so powerful, human beings like us must seem like maggots to him."

This was a truly terrible thing for Job to hear. How could he have caused the death of his own children? What on earth was Bildad talking about? He longed to talk to God face-to-face and tell him that he thought he'd been very unjustly treated.

Zophar, the third friend, was no better than the others. He, too, thought God was punishing Job for being wicked. "He will vent his blazing anger on you," he said. "And he will hail blows on you for what you have done."

Job stuffed his fingers into his ears so he couldn't hear anymore. "This is *useless!*" he yelled at his three so-called friends. "Why can't you have pity for me? You can see what God has done."

For a while the four men sat in silence on the heap of ashes.

Then Job plucked up all his courage. He was going to tell God exactly what he was feeling. None of the others had dared to do that.

"What have I done to displease you, Lord?" he asked. "What have I done to you? Just look at me. I'm covered with sores from head to foot and my breath is bad and my skin's all peeling away. Lord, I just want to die."

But God did not reply, so Job continued to sit on the ash heap.

As the awful silence got longer and longer, he turned to his three friends and said, "God is ignoring me. He may be passing by, but I certainly can't see him. Why doesn't he answer?"

"Lord," he began again, turning back to the silent, invisible God, "you know everything about me. You formed me as I lay in my mother's womb. So why do you shoot all these arrows into me? Why have you killed all my children and all my animals? Why, Lord? *Why?*" It felt very black inside Job's soul, and the blackness lasted for a very long time.

Then something happened that he did not understand. The awful darkness lifted for a moment. He felt he could breathe again, and he found himself saying, "I know that my Redeemer lives and that one day he will stand upon this earth. Even after death, when my skin has wasted away, I will still have a body, and I will see God with my own eyes."

But it was only after a lot more waiting and a lot more questioning that Job got an answer from God about why good people have to suffer. When this answer came, it was not at all as Job had expected—because God asked *him* questions.

God said, "Who are you to question my wisdom with your ignorant, empty words? Now stand up straight and answer the questions I ask you. Were you there when I made the world? If you know so much, tell me about it. Who decided how large it would be? Who stretched the measuring line over it? Do you know all the answers? Who holds up the pillars that support the earth? Who laid the cornerstone of the world? In the dawn of that day the stars sang together, and the heavenly beings shouted for joy.

"Look at all the wonderful things I have made," he said to Job. "I have made the sea and penned it in to control its fury. I have shaped the earth like a potter shapes clay. I have made storehouses for snow and hail. I have sprinkled the heavens with stars.

"I have made wild things like lions and mountain goats and eagles. I have made silly birds like ostriches, which lay their precious eggs where people will tread on them but which run faster than any horse and rider. I have provided the young raven with its food and I have watched over the wild deer as it gives birth. All things, great and small, are in my special care."

And Job thought hard about all this and began to see God in a different way from before. Now he saw a God who had created all kinds of strange and amazing things out of sheer love. This was a huge God who could not be fully understood, nor was he meant to be.

"I am unworthy of you," he said to God at last. "I am not going to say any more." But God had more to show him: Behemoth, a great creature like a hippopotamus, and Leviathan, which resembled a gigantic crocodile—two of his creatures that seemed quite beyond human understanding and control.

In the end Job realized that nobody could fully understand God. The Lord had shown him his greatness and his power, and in the face of these things Job fell silent. When at last he plucked up courage to speak again, he said this: "I know, Lord, that you are all-powerful, that you can do everything you want. You ask how I dare question your wisdom when I am so ignorant. I talked about things I did not understand, about marvels too great for me to know. You told me to listen while you spoke and to try to answer your questions. In the past I knew only what others told me, but now I have seen you with my own eyes. So I am ashamed of all I have said and repent in dust and ashes."

God did not leave Job sitting on the heap of ashes. He took away the horrible sores, and he gave him back his wealth, twice as much as before. Job had more sons and more daughters and many thousands of sheep, cattle, and oxen so that the second half of his life was even better than the first.

He never understood completely why the bad things happened to him. But he did understand through the way God dealt with him that God is full of mercy and grace.

> *Yahweh, my heart is not too haughty,*
>   *I do not set my sights too high.*
> *I have taken no part in great affairs,*
>   *in wonders beyond my scope.*
> *No, I hold myself in quiet and silence,*
>   *like a little child in its mother's arms,*
>   *like a little child, so I keep myself.*
> *Let Israel hope in Yahweh*
>   *henceforth and for ever.*

Psalm 131

The Angel Who Danced in Fire

*The story of the fiery furnace and how
right is stronger than wrong*

Nebuchadnezzar was the king of Babylon. He had laid siege to the city of Jerusalem, deposed its king, and brought some of the people he had captured back to his own country to serve him there. Among these were three youths called Shadrach, Meshach, and Abednego. They were clever young men, and the king appointed them to rule over the province of Babylon. In one way, however, they were very different from him. King Nebuchadnezzar worshiped many gods, but they were of the Jewish faith and worshiped only one.

Nebuchadnezzar ordered a huge statue to be built. It was to be nine feet wide and ninety feet tall and completely covered in gold. When it was finished, he had it set up on the plain of Dura outside the city, and he ordered everybody in his kingdom to come look at it. Wherever they were, they were summoned to the dedication of the king's monstrous gold statue, and along they came: the satraps, the prefects, the governors, and the judges. Everybody obediently gathered together on the plain of Dura.

Then a royal herald made an official announcement: "Hear ye, hear ye!" he cried. "You are all commanded to worship this statue. As soon as you hear the sound of the horn and the flute, the zither and the harp, the sound of the music, you must fall down and worship. This command is for everyone, for all people of every language on earth. If you do not obey, if you do not worship the image of gold set up here by King Nebuchadnezzar, then you will instantly be thrown into a blazing fiery furnace."

The music started, all the instruments began to play, and as soon as the people heard the zither and the harp and the noise of the pipes, they dutifully fell down and worshiped the king's great gold statue.

But there were spies at the royal court, astrologers who looked at the stars and claimed to see into the future. They came to Nebuchadnezzar and said, "O King, live forever!" Then they told him, "You have ordered everybody to worship your golden

statue whenever the music sounds, and you have said that anybody who disobeys you will be thrown into a blazing fiery furnace. Well, the three men you put in charge of the province of Babylon, the young Jews who call themselves Shadrach, Meshach, and Abednego, are paying no attention whatever to your royal command. They do not serve your gods, and they certainly do not worship your image of gold."

When he heard this, Nebuchadnezzar flew into a blind rage, and he commanded the three young men to be brought before him. "Shadrach, Meshach, Abednego," he hollered, "is it true that you do not serve my gods? Is it true that you do not worship my golden statue? From now on, when you hear the music—the sound of zither, lyre, and harp, of pipes, flute, and horn—if you will fall down and worship my statue, all will be well. But if you do *not*, you will be thrown immediately into a blazing fiery furnace, and what god will be able to rescue you then?"

Shadrach, Meshach, and Abednego did not hesitate before making their reply. They had always obeyed God's commandment that people should not worship idols and man-made images, and they were not going to disobey him now. They said, "O King,

we do not need to defend ourselves in this matter. If we are thrown into the furnace of blazing fire, then we know that our God can save us, that he can rescue us from your hand. But even if he does not save us, know this: we will not serve your gods and we will not worship this statue that you have set up."

"Very well," said Nebuchadnezzar. "You have had your chance, and you have thrown it away." And he immediately ordered the fires that heated the furnace to be increased in number so that it would be seven times hotter than before. Then he sent for some of the strongest soldiers in his army and ordered them to seize Shadrach, Meshach, and Abednego, bind them securely, and throw them into the fiery furnace. So they were tied up, still fully clothed, and hurled into the flames. The intense heat killed some of the soldiers as they threw the three young men to their deaths.

The king positioned himself by the mouth of the furnace to see what would happen, and what he saw astonished him. He leaped to his feet and said to his advisers, "Did we not tie up three men and throw them into the fire?"

And they replied, "There were indeed three men, Your Majesty."

"But *look*," cried Nebuchadnezzar. "I can see four men inside the furnace. They are walking about freely in the middle of the flames; they are not bound anymore. The flames are not hurting them, and the fourth man looks like an angel."

Then the king went right up to the flaming furnace and shouted, "Shadrach, Meshach, Abednego, servants of the most high God, come out here!" The three men obeyed him and stepped out of the furnace, and all the satraps and governors and royal advisers crowded around to see what had happened. The fire had not touched the young men in any way. Their bodies were not burned, their hair was not singed, and their clothes had not been scorched. They did not even smell like the fire.

Then Nebuchadnezzar opened his mouth. "Praise to the God of Shadrach, Meshach, and Abednego!" he cried. "He sent an angel to save them from the flames. They trusted him, and they were willing to die rather than worship another god. So this is my new decree. Anyone in the world who says anything against this God of theirs, I will have cut to pieces, and his house will be flattened. No other god can save like the God of Shadrach, Meshach, and Abednego." And he promoted the three young men and gave them more power than before.

The Big Fish and the Little Worm

The story of Jonah and what happened when
he refused to obey God's instructions

Jonah was a prophet, one of the people chosen by God to preach his message to those who had turned away from him. One day God said to Jonah, "Get up! Go to Nineveh, that great city, because its wickedness has come before my eyes."

But Jonah ran away from God. In fact, he went in the opposite direction, toward Tarshish. In the port of Joppa, he found a ship that was going to Tarshish, paid his fare, and went on board. The last thing he wanted to do was to rely on God or to obey his command. Most of all, he wanted to escape from God's presence.

Nevertheless, God stayed very close to Jonah, and when the ship was at sea, he sent a great wind. The storm was so violent that the ship almost broke apart. In terror, the sailors sank to their knees and cried for mercy, each one to his own god. To lighten the ship they threw the cargo over the side, yet the ferocious storm went on raging.

Jonah did not hear the storm. He had gone down below the deck and was fast asleep. The captain shook him awake. "How can you sleep?" he bellowed. "Get up! Call upon this God of yours. He might listen and save us."

There was a belief among sailors that bad luck at sea was caused by one of the people on board. To find out who was responsible for the storm, they cast lots. The lot fell upon Jonah, and they began to question. "What do you do?" they asked him. "Where do you come from? Which country do you live in? What race are you?"

Jonah replied, "I am a Hebrew, and I worship the God who made both land and sea."

"So why have you run away from him?" the sailors cried. They already knew that Jonah had fled from the presence of God, because he had admitted it.

While they were questioning him, the sea got rougher and rougher. The waves were as tall as mountains now. "What do we have to do to bring an end to this terrible storm?" the sailors asked Jonah.

"Pick me up and throw me overboard," he said. "It will die away if you do that. This storm is all my fault."

But the sailors were good people. They did not want Jonah to drown, so they did their best to get the boat back to land. But rowing was impossible—the sea was even rougher than before. Again they cried out for help, this time to the God Jonah worshiped. "Do not let us die for taking away this man's life," they cried. "Do not blame us, Lord, for the death of an innocent man. In sending this storm on us, Lord, you have done as you pleased."

And they threw Jonah into the sea. The minute they did this, the waters ceased from their raging, and all was calm again. Then the fear of God came upon the sailors. They offered sacrifices and made vows.

As for Jonah, the Lord had provided a great fish for him that came along and swallowed him whole, and he stayed inside it in perfect safety for three days and three nights.

Deep inside the fish it was as dark as death. It felt like being in a tomb, but Jonah, knowing that God had shown mercy on him, prayed this prayer:

"I was about to die.

So I cried to you,

and you heard my voice.

You threw me into the sea.

The deep sea was all around me.

Seaweed wrapped around my head.

But you saved me from death,

Lord my God. . . .

When my life had almost gone,

I remembered the Lord."

Jonah promised to keep faith with God from then on. "I will make sacrifices to you," he said, "and what I have promised I will carry out." Then the Lord, hearing that Jonah was no longer trying to escape from his presence, commanded the fish to release Jonah from the darkness. And it opened its mouth and spewed him up onto dry land.

Then the word of the Lord came to Jonah once again: "Go to the great city of Nineveh and proclaim my message." This time Jonah obeyed, traveling at once to Nineveh, which was indeed a huge place, to carry God's message about the wickedness of its people. Walking straight into the city, he proclaimed, "Within forty days Nineveh shall be overthrown!"

The people believed this message from Jonah's God, and immediately they began to fast to show that they were truly sorry. Everybody gave up eating, and everyone, high

and low, rich and poor, put on sackcloth and ashes, which was another sign of repentance. The king himself rose up from his throne, set aside his kingly robes and put on sackcloth too. Then he sent out a royal decree saying that all people throughout the city must fast and wear sackcloth and ask God to forgive them, not just human beings, but animals also. Every living thing in that city was urged to turn away from evil and violence. "Who knows?" said the king of Nineveh. "God may relent even now and turn his anger into mercy."

And God, seeing that the Ninevites were doing all they could to repent, had compassion upon them. He had planned to destroy them, but he changed his mind.

Jonah was angry when he saw that God had spared Nineveh. It was not only renowned for its wickedness, but it was also a Gentile city. He wanted God's favor to be reserved for Hebrews like him. That was why he had run away from the Lord in the first place. "I knew this would happen," he said petulantly. "I knew you were a God full of compassion, slow to get angry and always ready to forgive. Take away my life. I would rather die than live."

But God said, "Have you any right to be angry?"

Jonah sulked. In silence he took himself off to a place outside the city, where he sat and waited to see what was going to happen.

The sun beat down, and it became very hot. God, still loving Jonah, provided a leafy vine as a shelter from the heat and Jonah was glad. But the next day, God sent a worm along to chew the vine to pieces so that it withered and died. Now Jonah's shelter was gone. Then God did something even worse. He sent a scorching wind that beat down so hard upon the prophet's head that he started to feel faint. This made Jonah furious, and he addressed God very angrily. "It would be better for me to die," he repeated.

"But do you have any right to be angry about the vine?" God asked him.

"Indeed I do," Jonah spat out. "I am so angry I could die with rage."

Then God explained to Jonah what he was trying to teach him. "You were concerned about the vine because it sheltered you, even though it sprang up

overnight and died overnight—a thing of no importance. Do you not see that I, the Lord God, have much more reason to be concerned about Nineveh, that great city, whose people are so ignorant they can hardly tell their right hand from their left; Nineveh, where there are more than 120,000 people and also many animals. Should I not spare them too?"

In this way, Jonah learned that God was the God of all, a God who would always spare those who repented and turned back to him in faith. Jonah wanted the people of Nineveh to perish, but God made him see how selfish he was being. The Lord's mercy is for everybody.

Where can I go to get away from your Spirit?

Where can I run from you?

If I go up to the skies, you are there;

If I lie down where the dead are, you are there.

If I rise with the sun in the east,

and settle in the west beyond the sea,

even there you would guide me.

With your right hand you would hold me.

I could say, "The darkness will hide me.

The light around me will turn into night."

But even the darkness is not dark to you.

The night is as light as the day.

Darkness and light are the same to you.

Psalm 139:7–12

A Shepherd and His Sheep

*The story of the lost sheep, which Jesus told
for anyone who has ever felt lost and alone*

Jesus told many stories to explain what God was like. This story was told to some people who were saying bad things about God.

"There was once a shepherd who had a hundred sheep. Most of them stuck together, as sheep do, but one of them had a will of her own and kept wandering off. One day, when the shepherd counted his sheep, he could only reach ninety-nine. So he counted them again, then again. But he always stopped at ninety-nine. One sheep was definitely missing.

"Although there were dangers—wild animals that might creep out of the shadows and carry a sheep or two away for its supper—the shepherd did not hesitate. He took his crook and set off across the hills to find the sheep that was lost.

"After he spent many hours walking, prodding at thickets with his crook, looking in caves, and calling the sheep's name across wild, empty places, he heard a pathetic little cry. It was a cheeping noise, more like a bird than a sheep, a noise rather like the cry of a newborn baby. It was coming from somewhere above his head.

"The shepherd had come to some rocks. Leaving his crook on the ground, he began to climb, and as he got higher and higher, the bleating sound got louder. At last, marooned on a rock just above him, too frightened to jump or to find an easier way down, was his little lost sheep. 'Come on,' the shepherd said gently, and steadying himself below her, he reached out his arms and carried her to safety. Then, draping her across his broad shoulders (she was nearly asleep), he set off on the long journey home.

"The other shepherds had missed him. They jeered as he trudged into sight with the tiny sheep slung across his back. 'You left ninety-nine good sheep for *her!*' they said. 'Was it really worth it?'

"But the good shepherd took no notice. 'Rejoice with me,' he said as she scampered off to join the others. 'I have found the one sheep that was lost.'

"And that is what God is like," said Jesus. "He never gives up on us, however far away we wander from his side. When a sinner comes back to God, there is great, great happiness—far more than there would be over ninety-nine good people, who keep all the rules and never need rescuing!"

The Enemy Who Became a Friend

*The story of the good Samaritan, which Jesus told
to show how people should treat one another*

People who were jealous of Jesus sometimes tried to trick him. One day a man who knew all about the law came to him and asked, "Teacher, what must I do if I want to gain eternal life?"

"What does the law say?" replied Jesus.

At once the man quoted it by heart: "'Love the Lord your God with all your heart and with all your soul and with all your mind and with all your strength' and, 'Love your neighbor as yourself.'"

"You have given the right answer," Jesus told him. "Do these things and you will gain eternal life."

Trying to be clever, the man then said to Jesus, "But who is my neighbor?"

This is how the Lord replied.

"Once upon a time, a man was traveling from Jerusalem to Jericho, and on the loneliest part of the road, where thieves hang out, some robbers swooped down on him. They stripped him of his clothes, beat him up, and ran away, leaving him half-dead.

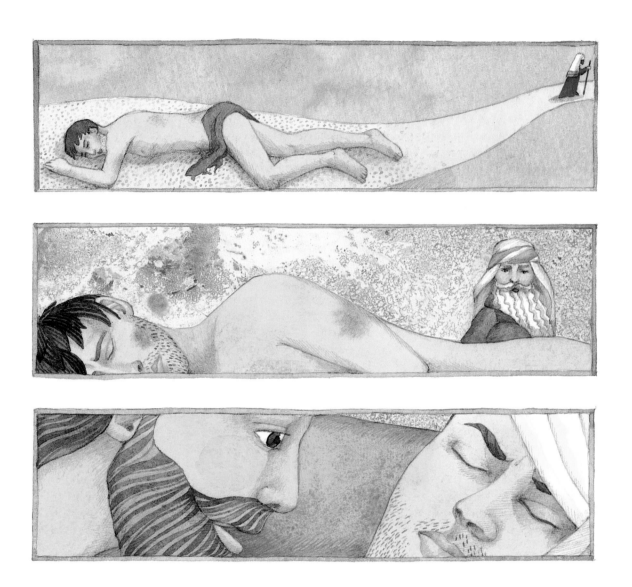

"As it happened, a priest soon came along, but when he saw the poor man lying there naked and bleeding, he crossed over to the other side of the road and went on his way. A little later, a Levite came by. He too was a holy man, from the tribe of Levi, and he did exactly the same thing. Seeing the poor man half-dead in the baking heat, he gathered up his robes and passed swiftly over to the other side of the road before hurrying on his way.

"The third person to come along the road was a Samaritan. Samaritans were detested in that country. No one ever looked to the Samaritans for help. But as soon as he saw the traveler sprawled in the dust, this man hurried over to him. When he saw what the robbers had done, his heart was filled with compassion.

"He poured oil and wine on the man's wounds to ease the pain, and he bandaged them. Then he managed to get the man onto his own donkey. He took him to an inn and stayed with him all night and looked after him.

"In the morning he had to be on his way, so he went to the innkeeper, took two silver coins from his purse, and said, 'Take care of him and, if you spend more than this, I will pay you when I come back.'

"Now then," Jesus said to the man who had questioned him about the law, "which of the three travelers was a neighbor to the man who fell among thieves?"

"The one who showed mercy on him," came the reply.

Then Jesus said, "Go and do the same."

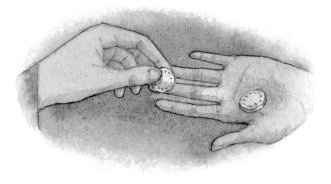

The Seed That Falls

*The story of the grain of wheat
and why death is not the end*

Jesus knew that he would die, that his enemies would plot against him and that he would be nailed to a cross. But he knew also that God his Father would raise him from the dead. As the time of his death approached, he comforted his friends by telling them what happens in the world of nature.

"If a grain of wheat falls to the ground and dies," he said, "that single grain seems to wither away—there is nothing left of it. But what actually happens is different from what people think. The single grain of wheat becomes a plant, and that new plant produces hundreds of seeds. The wheat has not died at all. It has taken on a new life, a life that is richer and fuller than the one it had before."

Then he said to his special friends, the disciples, "Those people who love their lives in this world will not be like the wheat seed. They will die, and that will be the end of them. But the people who follow me and are willing to serve me, even if it means giving up their lives, will pass into eternal life; they will never die."

Later, Jesus' followers repeated his teaching. In a letter, Paul wrote, "Someone may ask, 'How are the dead raised? What kind of body will they have?' This is my answer: when you plant something, it must die in the ground before it can live and grow. And when you plant it, what you plant does not have the same 'body' that it will have later. What you plant is only a seed, maybe wheat or something else. But God gives it a body that he has planned for it.

"It is the same with the dead who are raised to life. The body will decay, but that body is raised to a life that cannot be destroyed."

The City of Gold

A dream of heaven

The last book of the Bible is called Revelation, and it is full of the amazing things that God's Holy Spirit revealed to a follower of Jesus named John. This is what it tells us.

"It was an angel who sent me this vision. It happened to me, John, when I was on the island of Patmos on the Lord's Day.

"I heard a great voice like a trumpet, and it said, 'Write on a scroll what you see, and send it to the seven churches.' So I turned around and there behind me was someone like the Son of man. He wore a golden girdle and a robe that swept the ground. His head and his hair were white, like wool or new-fallen snow, and his eyes were like blazing fire. His voice sounded like the rushing of many waters, and he held seven stars in his right hand. Out of his mouth came a two-edged sword, and his face shone like the sun in all its glory.

"This sight was too much for me to bear, and I fell at his feet as if dead. But the Son of man stretched out his hand and said, 'Do not be afraid. I am the First and the Last. I was dead but now I am alive forever and ever, and I hold the keys to death and hell.'

"After this I saw many visions. I saw an open door, and through the door was heaven. Whoever sat on the throne of heaven was ablaze with light and the colors of precious stones like jasper, carnelian, and emerald. In front of this throne unrolled a great sea and the water was as clear as glass.

"Around the throne I saw four creatures, and their bodies were covered with eyes. One was like a lion and another like an ox. The third had the face of a man, and the fourth was an eagle. Day and night the creatures cried, 'Holy, holy, holy is the Lord God Almighty.' The being on the throne held a scroll in his hand, and an angel said in a mighty voice, 'Who is worthy to break the seals and open the scroll?' But nobody there was considered worthy, and I wept and wept.

"Then I saw the lamb, which looked as if it had been killed for sacrifice, yet was

alive, and it took the scroll from the hand of the heavenly being seated on the throne. Those around the throne sang, 'You are worthy to take the scroll and to open its seals because you died for everyone.'

"Then I saw a great crowd of people standing before the throne and before the Lamb, people of every nation on earth. They were dressed in white, and they held palm branches in their hands. They cried, 'God, who is the Father, and the Lamb have saved us from our sins.'

"I saw a new heaven and a new earth, because the first heaven and earth had passed away and there was no more sea. And I saw the new Jerusalem coming down from heaven from God, beautifully dressed, as a bride would dress for her husband.

"Out of heaven came a voice that said, 'Behold, the tabernacle of God is with men,

and he will dwell with them. They shall be his people, and God himself shall be with them and be their God. And God shall wipe away all tears from their eyes, and there shall be no more death, neither sorrow nor crying, neither shall there be any more pain.'

"And I saw a throne, and he who sat upon it said, 'Behold, I make all things new.'

"Then he said, 'Write: because these words are true and faithful.'

"And this is what I wrote down: 'It is done. I am Alpha and Omega, the beginning and the end. Anyone who is thirsty can come to me and drink from the fountain of the water of life. Those who are victorious over evil shall be rewarded. I will be their God, and they will be my children.'

"After this, I saw a river. It was as clear as crystal, and I knew that it was the water of life. It flowed from the throne and ran down the middle of the city street. On each

bank of the river I saw the Tree of Life, whose leaves bring healing to the nations. I know now that God is all-powerful and that the darkness of sin will never cover that city. There will be no need of lamps, not even the lamp of the sun itself. God will give everyone light, and he will reign forever and ever.

"It was I, John, who saw all these things, and when I had written all the visions down, I was about to shut the book. But the angel who had guided me said, 'No, the time is very near now.'

"And Jesus himself said, 'I am coming soon.'

"Let it be so. Come, Lord Jesus!"

Amen.

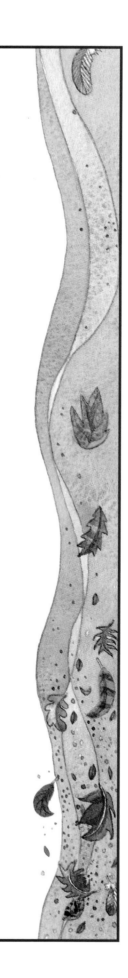

Index of Bible Passages

The stories in this book have been retold from the Bible.
The following references will enable you to look them up
in the Bible itself.

In the Beginning
Genesis 1–2

The Wily Serpent
Genesis 2:7–3:24

The Promise of the Rainbow
Genesis 6:1–9:17

The Tower That Reached to Heaven
Genesis 11:1–9

The Day Everything Went Wrong
The book of Job

The Angel Who Danced in Fire
Daniel 2:46–3:30

The Big Fish and the Little Worm
The book of Jonah

A Shepherd and His Sheep
Matthew 18:10–14; Luke 15:3–7

The Enemy Who Became a Friend
Luke 10:25–37

The Seed That Falls
John 12:24–26; I Corinthians 15:35–38, 42

The City of Gold
*Revelation 1:1–2, 10–18; 4; 5; 7:9–10; 21:1–7;
22:1–5, 8–10, 20*